# PICKING UP

Alexander García Düttman
Jean-Luc Nancy

RCA Photography 2010
Olivier Richon

## BOUNCING BACK

# PICKING UP

Alexander García Düttman
Jean-Luc Nancy

## COMING AND GOING

The students who are graduating this year have given me forty-two photographs. A question I ask myself when looking at these photographs is whether the students are coming to photography, whether photography is coming to them, as it were, whether they are going away and leaving photography behind, or whether photography has gone away and left them behind, transforming them into students baffled or exhilarated at the prospect of what could but will not always be a point of departure. Some photographs look like photographs of a mock set, a stage, an installation, a tableau; others look like photographs of first nature turned into second nature. Then there are photographs of photographs, photographs that seem to emerge out of a haze or merge into it, photographs that display dots to which the photographic objects have been reduced. Two tall buildings, white, grey, black, surrounded by blankness, appear as if they were models or ideas of buildings, a designer's dream, pure forms with only a remainder of reference: a reflection on the surface of one of the buildings is cut off from its origin but still draws an otherwise invisible outside into the photograph. One photograph I received folded, so that I don't see the animal looking at itself. The photographic image ceases to be a mirror. Where the photograph is abstract, it is not clear anymore whether photography must be considered an effect of technological manipulation, or whether, through abstraction, it affirms itself over the object. Once upon a time the beholder saw the photographed object first, then perhaps the photograph itself. In one case, photographs are replaced with whimsical, cartoonish drawings. A tumbling figure erects a tower around its own body. Has the photographer immured himself? There must have been a moment, though, when the students did not know if they were coming or going, if photography was coming to them or leaving them behind. Otherwise, how could they explain their desire to study photography? The one who desires photography wishes to be surprised by it. What remains of photography once it is gone, once it is no longer coming, is its concept, the result of one's studies. Many of the photographs I see here appear to be on the border between photography and the concept of photography, as if, knowingly or unknowingly, the students asked themselves, can photography still photograph its concept, or does the concept undo photography?

**Stuart Bailes**
*The Movement of Things*
*Photograph I*

## IDEAS

I would willingly extend this remark by saying that
all the photographs – some of which are in fact at the
limits of photography – seem to me to carry meaning,
or signification. It is not that they always refer to
the concept of photography, even if this is necessarily
implicated in every case. Rather, they refer to concepts
such as the ones I have used here: the passage or the
access, touch, weight. It is for this reason, then, that I
have chosen to anchor my notes in ideas more than in
the forms, manners, or styles of the photographs in
question. In fact, not having a teaching relationship with
the creators of these images as Alex does, I didn't even
have in mind that these students were studying
photography. I neglected that fact in favour of viewing
the photographs as a random selection of images, which
were for me not even necessarily a collection of 'images'
but rather of 'documents'. At times, they 'document' a
procedure, or a specific effect – a procedure that can be
visual or narrative or amount to a witticism. At times,
they do seem to want to create an image, but this image
foregrounds precisely its character as a representation of ...
something: of an intention or a proposition, of something
that calls for comprehension or interpretation.

## MASS, AMASSED WEIGHT, PILED UPON ITS OWN GRAVITY

This has fallen (4)[1]. It didn't surge up, it didn't rise up above
the earth. It is the earth itself. The earth fallen in upon
itself, a fall pure and simple. The world is born in this fall,
during which the sharp air, the vivid, bracing air, which
for its part never ceases to climb, slices the falling mass and
divides it into distinct terrains.

## EARTHQUAKE

The buildings have ceased to give shelter. Look at the
broken glass with a razor-sharp edge (4). But the fear of
the earth collapsing into, and falling onto, itself, seems
contained now that the catastrophe has happened and
that we know that it will happen again. The deadly and
indifferent light shining from above contains it.

[1] A number within brackets
indicates a page number.
The reader will find the
photograph referred to in
the text by looking at the
page thus indicated.

## PASSAGE, PASSAGEWAY, NARROW PATH, SECRET ACCESS – BUT TO WHAT?

Perhaps to a stage where, exiting from the wings, you suddenly find yourself (7). There, you would perform a play whose script you would have to make up on the spot. Or, as if exiting from a theatre or perhaps a tent, it may just as well lead to an outside, towards a dazzling exterior. The curtains veil its intensity. In the end, it is this intensity that you want to reach, even at the risk of being burned.

**Stuart Bailes**
*The Movement of Things*
*Photograph II*

## TENT

Photography needs to build a tent (7), or else the traces
will disappear in the whiteness of cold light. Hence the
intensity felt when following the traces, when looking
at a photograph.

### LET US GO VISIT THE SAGE ON THE MOUNTAIN! LET US GO!

We know it well: the sage is there, in his shelter on the
mountain (8). On our misty sojourn, we hope to be able
to reach him one day and receive his advice. But perhaps
this voyage has always already begun, perhaps it is never
finished. We never arrive, but we journey nonetheless.
Every day we begin anew.

**Savinder Bual**
*Myriorama*

**Alejandro Guijarro**
*Sea*

## NEITHER HERE NOR THERE

I know that I must leave the city, where nothing ever
comes into focus because my eyes are constantly distracted.
I know that I will be able to concentrate and see something
only if I reach the surrounding hills after crossing the river
and climbing through the low clouds (8). And yet I also
know that it will be the same over there, and that it is here
that I need to seek sharpness. If I cannot find it here, I will
not find it there.

**LOST FROM SIGHT, VANISHED, FAR OFF, VERY FAR OFF**
So far off that peering into the distance the eyes lose
themselves (11, 9). Not only is there no longer anything
to see, there is no more view. No more vision, no more
viewing, no more viewer. What is left are only the black
or white depths of the absolutely distant – and also the
eyes, our eyes, turned towards this distance, dazzled,
enucleated spectators.

**'MÄRCHENWALD'**
I was still a child when I realised that my fairy-tale forest
(11) was doomed because it did not extend indefinitely.
Of course the very fact that I could access it, leave the
house and go there, meant that its extension was limited.
But going to the fairy-tale forest was not like going to
a nature reserve. Then my grandfather told me of the plans
to build a highway in the vicinity of the Hunter's Fountain.
That's when the forest turned fake.

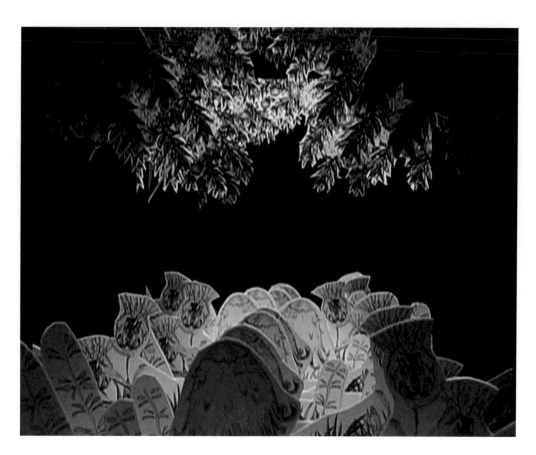

**Savinder Bual**
*Follis Arboreus,* film still

## 12 AND 13 – TOGETHER: IS THAT WHICH CEMENTS ELEMENTS TO EACH OTHER IN AN ASSEMBLAGE ITSELF ALSO PART OF THE ASSEMBLAGE?

Or rather: the lesson of deconstruction. Deconstruction consists in disassembling a construction, which supposes first of all that one can remove that which assembles the construction, that which cements it, glues it, joins or ties it together. The assemblage remains, but disassembled, in pieces, on its way to chaos. To remove that which joins the parts together is to remove the 'con'.[2] What is left is the 'struction'. In French, this word once designated a mound, a pile, a heap without order. The pure structure, but as yet unstructured.

[2] In French, 'con' also means 'stupid' – trans.

**Diana Fiedler**
Opposite: *Interior #1.*
Interior constructed from the
exterior of a housing estate
tower block
Below: *Unit*
Interior constructed from the
exterior of a housing estate
tower block

## OUT OF JOINT

The photographer can make an image by taking a snapshot. Or he can make an image by putting it together artificially. All the other options available to him depend on the possibility of there being such a choice. However, this possibility is not the same as the possibility of a deconstruction of photography. Rather, the possibility of a deconstruction of photography lies in the experience of a necessity that renders choice obsolete. The photographer who deconstructs photography, for instance by exploiting the resources of an artificial fabrication of the image, does so out of necessity, not because he chooses to do something he could just as well not do (12, 13).

## SAND, DUST, GRANULATION, PULVERULENCE, MINISCULE INFINITY

Just as grains of sand on the beaches and deserts run between the fingers of those who want to grasp them (15), so we escape, become invisible, hide ourselves. Thus are we all dispersed, all together, living and dead, animals and plants, seas, mountains, and grains of sand.

## SCATTERED ASHES

If there is an ability that humans can perfect into an art, it is the ability never to be fully there. Survival lies in escape; death is nothing but a final distraction. Does the photographer's task then not consist in creating an image that captures the ability of artful humans, and even testifies to it (15)?

**Alejandro Guijarro**
*Desert*

**Sarah Mei Herman**
*Jana and Feby, April 2009*

## TOUCH: TACT, CONTACT, CONTAGION

How good it is to touch (**16, 17!**) How dangerous it is!
Suddenly, in the silence and in a backward glance, or a
glance that is too close, too absorbed, I vibrate with the
vibration of another body, of other matter. What makes
itself known here, what presses upon me and I press upon,
is a consistency, a density, a bearing, an allure. This pressure,
this eagerness, concentrates my entire presence into the
parts that are in contact. Everything else disappears,
faints, vanishes.

## SEEING AND TOUCHING

In one photograph (16), two girls hug, touch each other,
though the lost gaze of the girl who is leaning against
a wardrobe seems to detach her whole body from the
embrace. In the other photograph (17), a girl lies on an
empty field and her entire body touches the soil, though
is she herself being touched as she listens to the rumours
of the earth? When I hold a photograph in front of my
eyes in order to look at it, I am rarely aware of the fact
that I am actually touching it. Sometimes people touch
the photograph of a loved one, caress the image of a face,
place the tip of their fingers on photographed eyes or lips.

**Amit Nachumi**
*Harvester*

**Frederic Huska**
*Back to a Dead End,*
*1st Street, Brooklyn*

## VIA RUPTA: BROKEN PATH, AND THE ORIGIN OF 'RUE'[3] OR OF 'ROAD'[4] ; A RUPTURE THAT OPENS THE PASSAGEWAY, A FAULT, A BREACH

Not a pathway traced by the regular passage of men and animals through the fields, the woods, even the rocks, but instead an opening or clearing that decisively points the way across the country (18). Borders form along the path of this rupture, borders along which buildings can eventually arise. Here one does not travel to and fro between places, but resolves to move forward with full force, in full flight.

[3] In French, 'rue' means 'street' – trans.

[4] English in original – trans.

### GOOGLE

Is the difference between the way that needs to be paved for there to be a world, and the road that connects two neighbourhoods in a city, the same as the difference between the usage an artist makes of photography and the usage an Internet surfer makes of an interactive map with street views? Yes, unless one is able to travel from one point of the city to another as if for the first time (18), or unless one is able to take the pictures that one is looking at as if they did not yet exist.

### IVORY TOWER, THE NECK OF SHULAMITH, A TOWER REMOVED FROM THE WORLD, REJECTED, EXILED

A precious substance, once called elephantine, reputed
to be of a perfect whiteness and of a singularly unctuous
hardness, a mine full of jewels, of coral or gemstones. Who
knows how it became the material of a tower where those
who withdraw from the world, who disdain the world or
quite simply ignore it, isolate or even enclose themselves?
Every tower becomes an ivory tower – but the elephants,
they disappear. (20, 21, 22)

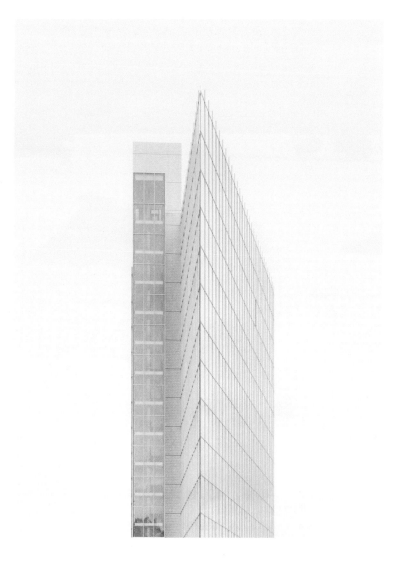

**Agata Madejska**
Opposite: *Ideogram 004*
Above: *Ideogram 006*

## WHITE ELEPHANTS

Why do ivory towers (**20, 21, 22**) have such a bad reputation?
Does one not need an image to discover the world?
Without such an image, the world swallows me and I make
no discoveries at all. Photography tells me not to be afraid
of the ivory tower. That's the place where the portrait of the
photographer as an artist is made.

**Darragh O'Callaghan**
*Brickbuilded*

## A SAW: CUTTING, POINTED TEETH, JIGSAW, SCREECHING, HISSING

The sky has been carved up, it has been sawed into pieces
(**24**). The horizon has been transformed into teeth and
slicing blades. It is forbidden to think beyond this horizon:
we are consigned to this circle carved out of the sky. You
can feel the fangs tear into the image and rip it to shreds.

**Melanie Rozencwajg**
*Liverpool Street Station,*
*Sunday 5pm – 5:30pm,*
*Flow of People*

**Melanie Rozencwajg**
*Periphery*

**REPRIMAND**
You have been biting your fingernails (**24**).

## AUTHORITY

'Authority' is a word I picked up after Francette had used
it. She was trying to make sense of a huge photograph
that showed a dirty and uneven white surface (**27**). One
could have confused it with a painted wall in an art
gallery. The wall's surface featured three holes and several
lines drawn with a pencil. Now I have a close-up, or
a magnified detail, of this wall on my desk (**26**). Tomorrow
I will be told that the actual photograph consists of a large
number of smaller photographs but I do not know it
yet. I look at the wall and see a mark, probably to
pinpoint the spot where a fourth hole will be added. Is
this the place where an oversized photograph will hang?
To give authority to something means to turn it into
something that will be able to impose itself. Here, the
wall imposes itself upon the viewer like a fact because
the photograph achieves a *trompe l'oeil* effect. But a *trompe
l'oeil* also undermines the authority it gives. And the
photographed absence of a photograph does the same:
it gives authority to photography as it undermines it. Is
photography a puppet?

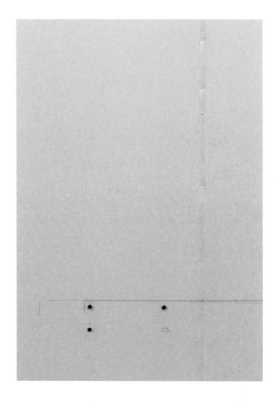

**Soon-Hak Hwon**
Right: *History of* Espace Cinq
Etoiles *No. 5* (detail)
Opposite: *History of* Espace
Cinq Etoiles *No. 5*

## MASK

In image (**27**), I see something else. There is a surface that
seems to be a large piece of cardboard, judging from
the detail provided by image (**26**), that is, from the pencil
line and the sort of creasing or alteration of the surface
perpendicular to the pencil line. It is attached to what looks
like a casing or housing. The piece of cardboard masks it.
Or maybe not. Nevertheless, at the base of the image,
a thick electrical conduit coming from the floor pushes
up into the casing behind the cardboard. So the cardboard
does hide something, after all – a lighting fixture, an
appliance. Or perhaps what could have been a lamp.

**Frederic Huska**
*Remember II*

## DÉJÀ-VU

I feel that I have already been there although I know that
I have not. What is it that triggers such a feeling? In one
photograph (28), it is the slope that becomes steeper just
beyond the red light, there where the road bends sharply
and I cannot look ahead. If this photograph were part
of an interactive map, I would click my mouse, go down
the street and turn right, so as to discover where I am.
In the other photograph (18), my feeling is triggered by
the trees at the end of the gently rising road. They block
the horizon. It is dark up there, and that's why the driver
of the car that is coming down towards me has switched
on the headlights. I know that, if I were to walk up to the
trees, I would hit St Kilda Road, and yet I am certain that
both photographs were made in America, not in Australia.
As if in a dream, this artist is aware of what I say to a
photographer: 'Connect me and disconnect me at the
same time.'

## DOUBLE EXPECTATION

'Déjà-vu', that is also exactly what I thought when looking
at these photographs (18, 28). That is why I went in the
direction of the via rupta, towards the question of the road
or the route. But the 'déjà-vu' was occasioned for me not
by the landscape, but rather by the photograph itself as a
photograph of a road. Photographs of roads or streets form
in some ways an autonomous genre. In such photographs,
everything takes place as if the opening of the pathway
provided a perspective for the photograph – a ready-made
and almost inevitable linear perspective. The street or the
road does nothing more than confirm a double expectation.
On the one hand, there is the expectation of the tracing,
of the vanishing lines, of parallels meeting in infinity: an
entire visual order is produced. On the other hand, there
is the expectation of the event: something can come to
pass on this road. People come and go. They cross, too. The
buildings on the sides of the road are there as borders only.

**Sidsel Christensen**
Below: *Light Girls,* video still
Opposite: *About the Light Surface
of Josephine Ditlev,* video still

### 'C'EST LA NUATE!'

The waves seem to have solidified into small soft cushions
that form an undulating rope along the beach, and even
if the photograph had not been taken on a beach but on
a frozen surface that prevents a wooden stick from sinking
into the water, the overall effect would still be one of
softness (9). A photograph, no matter how sharp, is a wad
of cotton wool placed between me and the world. The
world is wrapped in photography, and if you unwrap it,
little ashen grains fall into your hands and leave a trace on
your skin before they dissolve. This is what remains of the
nightclub. In the background, immersed in pink and blue
shadows, a girl displays her nose, her lips, her tits, her legs,
her arms (31). In the foreground, the flashes of light function
as the body's signals.

## THE SONG OF THE STYRENE

Cotton ... yes, and all sorts of other materials that can wrap things up and yet still allow me to see them: tulles, plastics, foams, or even polystyrene, which, once incorporated into reality, gives it a tense and fragile surface throughout.

**Darren Harvey-Regan**
*Heidegger's Lizard*

## A PHILOSOPHICAL GAG

The stone exerts pressure on the soil but that's not the
relation that the lizard has to it when it lies on the stone's
warm surface and exposes its body to the sun. Yet, the
philosopher tells us that we should cross out the words we
are using here, for, while relating to the stone in a way in
which the stone never relates to the soil, the animal still
does not relate to the stone as a stone. The things here are
'lizard things' and we wouldn't know what to call them.
There is no naming such things. Does it make a difference
whether the lizard lies on the stone or under it (**32**)? Only
if, instead of being crushed by the stone, it were trying
to lift it. But that's not a thing lizards do, as far as I know.
A photograph is a 'human thing', they might say when
looking at us, though we have no name to identify them,
don't even know if they have names which they must cross
out when referring to photographs. Can what we do with
and to photographs make a difference, then?

## STUDIO

To my mind, the question is this: why is this scene (**32**)
deprived of any environment? It takes place in the studio;
therefore nothing is happening here. The lizard is thus not
'poor in world' but entirely 'without world'. In fact, only
the stone is in a philosophical position here – after all, the
title of the photograph wants us to situate it in relation
to philosophy – and the lizard is but an appendage to the
stone, as mineral as the stone.

### THE CORNER OF MY EYE

When I see something out of the corner of my eye, my
vision is peripheral. Peripheral vision is good at detecting
motion, I read online. Hence making a video means
seeking motion detected in the uncertain margins of sight,
there where something rushes off stage and vanishes like a
ghost. As it accelerates, or as I start moving faster and faster,
the thing contracts, becomes smaller and smaller (**24**).
A video-camera is the eye of my *rückenfigur*.

## DIS-APPEARING

Essentially, yes, it disappears. It dis-appears [*disapparaît*],
I might say, but can such a word be translated into English?

## HEAVY

The Father has come out of the bushes and looks down
at the boy whose lowered head leans against him (35). The
boy's eyes are shut, and his arms hang heavily from his
shoulders. The Father does not touch the boy, hides his
hands firmly in the pockets of his trousers. Are the two
praying, asking for forgiveness? Here the artist has not shied
away from photography but has tackled it head-on, taking
the bull by its horns. It's all there and filled with presence.
Don't let photography get you down (17) when it exposes
the guilt, the fact that bodies and things take up space and
hence impose themselves, excluding other bodies and
other things from coming into existence, or from coming
to the fore. As I remember it, Werther feels guilty because
of all the destruction he causes simply by taking a walk
in the open space of nature. The reluctance so many
students experience in the face of photography may be
a recoiling from this truth, the truth photography reveals,
the truth of the guilt that haunts presence. They seek an
alliance with sense instead.

**Sarah Mei Herman**
*Julian and Jonathan, July 2009*

## 'DÍAS DE CAMPO'

But the girl lying on the ploughed earth (17) is not guilty.
She is alone only because the earth was just ploughed.
She is waiting for seedtime, and then the sprouting of the
crops and then the harvest. After that, she will no longer
be visible. She will be hidden by the stalks, while that huge
pale sky will be covered with the ears of wheat or corn.
That, at least, is what can be understood from what we
are given to understand.

**Noémie Goudal**
Below: *Passage*
(from the series *Island*)
Opposite: *Les Amants (Cascade)*

## SPILLING, SPINNING

A photograph is first nature as second nature, even in the
age of the digitisation of photography. Who, upon hearing
the word 'photography', would not think, for a moment at
least, of the photographic image as the trace of something
out there? Second nature is inserted in first nature and
carries it away (**37**). No one will muffle the clicking noise
made by the camera, and stop the spilling and flowing
of clichés. Could this not be the setting for a fashion shoot?
If fashion is the discovery of sex in art, it multiplies the
*quid pro quos*. The sad boy has lost his friend, or perhaps his
future self, to the beautiful young model who is sailing on a
sea of dead leaves as she turns her back on the glamourless
photograph of a landscape (**36**). The other boy has turned
the paintings so many times, has made them gyrate so
quickly, that their phantoms unravel as photographs and
their colours are filtered into a series of monochromes (**38**),
(**39**). There is a family resemblance between these phantoms.
Beauty here is of the idea.

**Luke Turner**
Above: *The Annunciation,*
*Sandro Botticelli*
Opposite: *The Mocking of Christ,*
*Fra Angelico*

## GHOST

Photography can also steal from the model a ghost, a
layer, a film of himself. Balzac was convinced that every
photograph lifted away a tiny quantity of being from its
subject. Therefore he refused to be photographed too
frequently. What we see in photographs of him is indeed
what remains of his body.

## HOOKER

The German word '*Höcker*' translates into English as
hump or hillock, not as hooker. The image to my left shows
Tuscan or Indian hills drawn with a pencil or a crayon (8),
the image to my right a tuft of hair placed in a corner (40).
Though the hair looks as if it were about to be served on a
plate, it resists such offering. Photography takes her punters
on a bumpy ride, no matter how polished and smooth the
surface of the prints may be. This punter has come from Ice
Station Zebra (41) equipped with an extra load (42). Bugger!

**Ewa Axelrad**
*INODOROUS*

**Joshua Bilton**
*Revolt in Owiu*

## PUSHING

The hair most certainly suggests the presence of a head (**40**).
However, it is not a question of serving these locks of hair
on a platter. Instead, the head is pushed into a corner, and
turned to face it, as is indicated by the position of the hair.
What pushes the head into a corner is yet another corner,
which threatens to crush it into the wall. Or is it perhaps
a photographer who is being pushed in this way?

**Joshua Bilton**
*Buckle*

## RESURRECTION

'The people who walked in darkness have seen a great
light: they that dwell in the land of the shadow of death,
upon them hath the light shined.' This is the confirmation
motto that was chosen for me. Here the light shines only
on the threshold, dimly illuminates the paving slabs or
a wall that blocks the path (**12, 13**). There the light is artificial
and isolates, for a moment only, the profile of a blond girl
absorbed in checking her mobile phone (**43 below**) while
the audience gathers around an empty stage (**43 above**).
How far and how deep must the camera penetrate into
micro- and macrocosm (**11, 44, 45**) to see the light, and for
the light to shine on it? Light and Photography are the
Great Resurrectors.

**Norma-Louise Thallon**
Above: *Downstairs at the King's
Head (18 minutes to performance)*
Below: *Downstairs at the King's
Head (6 minutes to performance)*

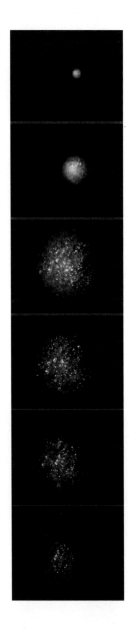

**Valerie Furnham**
*Propulsion*

Lauren Winsor
*Frôler*

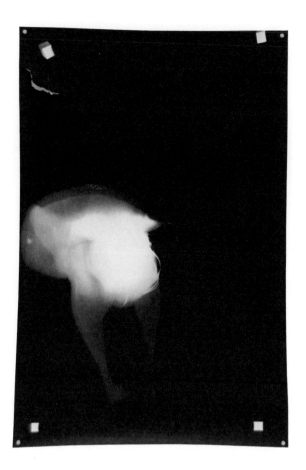

## OUT OF THE FRAME, OUT OF THE WORLD

Perhaps every photograph, no matter which, defines, intentionally
or not, a sort of cosmos that is at the same time a microcosm and a
macrocosm. A cosmos, because everything is ordered, everything is
arranged in the frame, which justifiably or not cuts off and excludes
everything that exceeds it. Whereas in a painting the contents of the
frame are composed or contained, in a photograph the frame cannot
prevent something from escaping it, from lying outside the frame,
something that comes to lie outside the very world. This cosmos
is a macrocosm because in a single stroke it configures a universe:
nothing here but these people, this sign reading 'Downstairs',
these microphones and these singers or actors who have not yet
appeared, these lamps like celestial lights and the question 'but what
is happening here?' (**43**). However, it is also a microcosm, because
the photographs retain all the folds of the clothing, the stains on
the wall, and above all the slow, interminable fading of the light
and the shadows.

**Una Hamilton Helle**
*Mot himmelrik*

**no**

The conspirators plot in a dark forest and Insurrection
rises into a white night (**46**). Where is Photography?
Underground. Can Peace rescue the naked boy (**36**) from
War? He searches so despondently for his own reflection
in the dead waters that Pornography wishes to abduct him.

**yes**

*Why not?* Isn't pornography essentially photographic?
Isn't it always a matter of seeing what isn't made to be seen,
and vice versa, you ask. Ask yourself.

# BOUNCING BACK

Olivier Richon

Coming and going; out of joint; ideas; earthquakes; white elephants; reprimand; mask; *déjà vu*. By writing about, around, and from photographs, Nancy and Düttmann have produced a series of fragments on photography that read perhaps like fragments of concepts. The way they arrived at these concepts is not through other concepts but through the students' photographic works. We could agree with Antonino, the hero of Calvino's short story, *The Adventure of a Photographer*, that 'perhaps true total photography is a pile of fragments'.[1] Dialogues are made of fragments, and fragments, like dialogues have neither an essential beginning nor end. Contingent and capricious, they do not bother about narrative continuity. And what is a photograph if not a fragment…

[1] Italo Calvino, *The Adventure of a Photographer*, in *Difficult Loves*. London: Picador, 1985.

**Joshua Bilton**
*Buckle,* detail

| | |
|---|---|
| SWARMING | MUTED |
| STICKY | HYGIENIC |
| DISHEVELED | TIGHT |
| PENETRABLE | NARROW |
| FILTHY | HAIRLESS |
| PROSTRATE | ERECT |
| GREASY | INODOROUS |
| CONTAGIOUS | RIGID |
| CHARRED | COOL |
| SMELLY | IMPERVIOUS |
| SAGGING | BLEACHED |

**Ewa Axelrad**
*Solution*

**Alejandro Guijarro**
*Chopped Tomatoes*

**Una Hamilton Helle**
*Nekrosus*
Video still

**Sidsel Christensen**
*Conversations with the Other Side*
Documentation from performance, video still

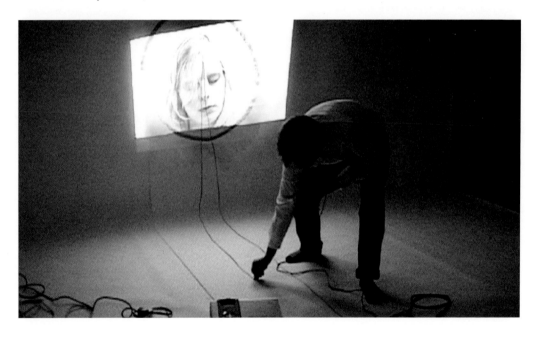

**Diana Fiedler**
*Interior #1*
Installation view

**Una Hamilton Helle**
*Leys*
Installation detail

**Stuart Bailes**
*Flank*

**Luke Turner & Nastja Rönkkö**
*Untitled*

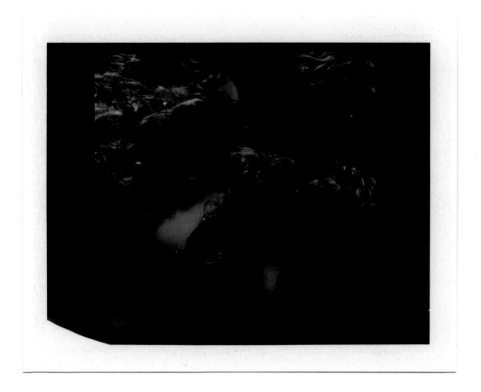

**Lauren Winsor**
*$20^2$*

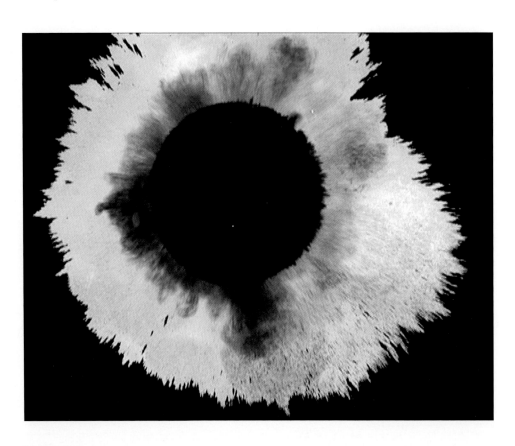

**Valerie Furnham**
*Fe2O3 = PLXNA2 = Anxiety*

**Darren Harvey-Regan**
*All The Logic of Which an Existence is Capable*
*– Albino Badger and Badger in a Bag*

**Savinder Bual**
*Follis Paluster*
Film still

**Noemie Goudal**
*Les Amants (Chaleur)*

Agata Madejska
*81 – 86*

**Sarah Mei Herman**
*Jonathan, October 2009*

**Amit Nachumi**
*The Gate Keeper*

**Amit Nachumi**
*Sabres*

**Frederic Huska**
*The Corner House*

**Darren Harvey-Regan**
*The Elsewhere Mouse*

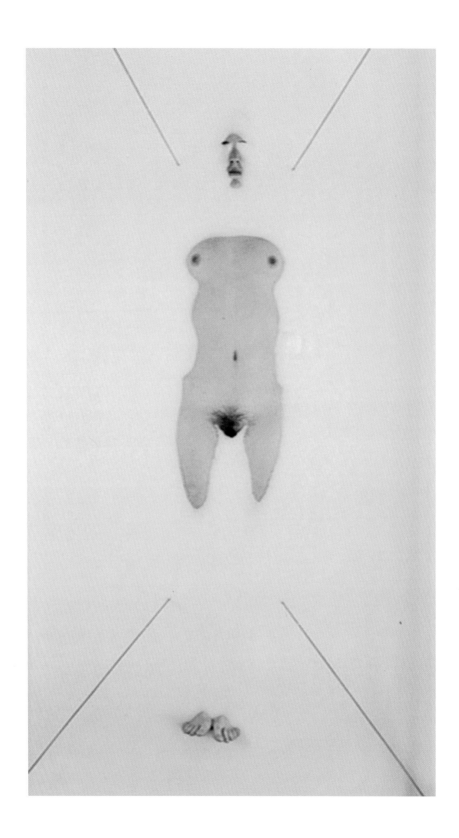

**Darragh O'Callaghan**
Above: *Jackhammered*
Opposite: *Untitled*

**Soon-Hak Hwon**
*History of Sesame Gallery*
Installation view

**Valerie Furnham**
*Scratch test = 1→2→4→8→16→32→∞ = Anticipation*

**Lauren Winsor**
*Automatic Poiesis*

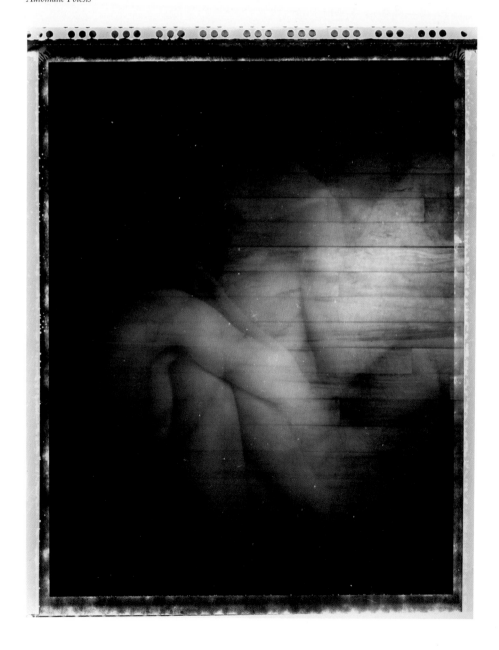

**Norma-Louise Thallon**
*Become a Master of Disguise*

**Melanie Rozencwajg**
*Untitled Document*

… It makes me bounce back to the few images that
illustrate Nicéphore Niépce's invention of photography.
Here is a minimal corpus of images: a portrait, a view from
a window and a dressed table. Are these more than just
material for experimentation? Are they thinking images?
An engraving made in 1650 of the profile of Cardinal
d'Ambroise is his subject for reproduction. In reproducing
by contact a seventeenth-century engraving, Niépce puts
duplication to the fore. He makes a picture from a picture, a
200-year-old engraving. He makes a photograph of culture,
an image of an image. But let us leave aside this cardinal and
its reproduction and reduce our corpus to just two images:
the window and the table.

Between 1816 and 1827, Nicéphore Niépce took
dozens of views with a camera obscura from his attic
window in Gras. True, the images were fading and he had
to constantly renew the experiment until he managed
to find a way of fixing them. Yet he never tired of this
view from a window as subject matter. The view from the
window is what Niépce calls the first photograph from
Nature. There is no landscape. Instead we see diagonal
lines, shadows and outlines of buildings and a horizon
which gives us a vanishing point and a certain perspectival
pull. The image is on a plate of pewter, as reflective as a
mirror, that shows the imprint of a faint and elusive image.

From Alberti onwards, we have inherited a notion that a painting or a picture is like a window, a window through which one sees the world. Gerard Wajcman reminds us that Alberti says something a bit different.[2] He writes that a painting is an open window through which we can look at the story. *Story* rather than world. This is quite a different emphasis. Alberti's window opens upon a text, a narrative. It opens upon a space where the visual and the textual are intertwined. Is Niépce's window also an aperture through which one has access to a story? Is it the story of a photograph, or a story that belongs to a general story of windows? Will window telling replace story telling? A window, Wajcman reminds us, is primarily a hole in the façade of a house. It lets the light in, it lets air in. A window does not necessarily involve looking. Yet how can one not look at a window? Isn't a window triggering our desire to look? The hole that is a window is not unlike a lens that lets the light into a camera. And some cameras use just this, pinholes, instead of lenses. What is a lens but a glazed hole? This type of hole produces an image, light forms an image, it does not simply illuminate in the manner of a window. Niépce named his image-making process heliography (sun drawing). We could call it holiography, and attach the image-making device of photography to the iconology of holes, or following Wajcman's argument, to hology, a discipline that would account for our knowledge of holes. It would deal with piercings, leakages, keyholes and openings of all sorts that facilitate and also threaten visibility. The eye is a type of hole, and so are the mouth, eyes, ears and nose; bodily holes may have something to do with vision and representation. The photographic image is from the outset determined by a hole and under threat of disappearing into one. The first experiments with light-sensitive substances did fail to fix the image, which would get darker and darker: an excess of light that darkens the image, just as the

[2] Gerard Wajcman, *Fenêtre, Chronique du regard et de l'intime (Window, Chronicle of the gaze and of the intimate).* Paris: Editions Verdier, 2004.

notorious black page in *Tristram Shandy* is an excess of ink that dissolves language.[3] The window of course is more than a hole; it is a framing device. Niépce claimed that his view from a window framed a piece of Nature. Why did it take him so long to get it right? Did he spend ten years looking out of his window, in idle fascination? At school, pupils with a tendency for reverie are kept away from windows. Windows can be closed or open, we see through them and we can be seen framed by them. Glass is used for windows and for early photographic plates. With a plate camera, the image is formed on a ground glass. Leonardo writes 'Of the plane of glass: perspective is nothing else than seeing a place (or objects) behind a pane of glass, quite transparent, on the surface of which the objects behind that glass are to be drawn.'[4]

[3] Laurence Sterne, *The Life and Opinions of Tristram Shandy*, Gentleman. London: Everyman's Library, 1912. Vol. 1, p. 25. The first two of this nine-part novel were first published in 1759.

[4] *The Literary Works of Leonardo da Vinci*. London: Phaidon, 1969. Vol. 1, p.150.

Kertész's broken glass plate of 1929 is printed decades later. It is a view from a high window it seems, looking above the rooftops and into a street of a European city. It is as if we are looking through a broken window, a window with a hole in it. We can see it and see through it.

The third image Niépce is known for is his table laid for a meal, this time a photograph on glass, probably made in 1829, according to the experts. The historians Helmut and Alison Gernsheim tell us that 'nothing remains of this still life but a rather poor halftone reproduction made in 1891'.[5] The original on glass was destroyed by a certain Professor Peignot, who 'seized one day with a fit of mania smashed everything in his laboratory, including his photographic incunabulum'. The image of the table seems to have been taken outside, against a wall, maybe the wall of the house with the attic window. It shows a table dressed for a meal. On the tablecloth we see a knife, perhaps, a spoon, a bottle of wine, a bowl on a plate, a wine glass with a stem, a piece of bread, I think, and a carafe. The wall has shadows that recall the shadows of the view from a window. This is a meal for a single diner. This is a picture for a single spectator. It is for me, who is looking at it now.

[5] Alison and Helmut Gernsheim, *The History of Photography*. Oxford: Oxford University Press, 1955.

The Gernsheims use the term *still life* for this picture. And still life is a genre that is particularly concerned with the frame. We move from the verticality of the window frame to the horizontality of a table that frames the objects that occupy its surface. The table is a horizontal frame that contains objects; within the still life genre, attention to the frame can be drawn, for instance, by placing a knife, a fruit or a vegetable at the edge. A tension is produced where the object hovers between the edge of the table and the frame of the picture. It comes out of the frame, as it were, thus making a bridge between the picture and the spectator.

Niépce's image is an awkward still life that depicts the moment before a meal is served. The absent food, the food yet to come, inscribes a future tense into the image. This is an ascetic, sober image that only consumes the light sensitive surface necessary for its making. It makes me think of Arthur Schopenhauer's famous attack on the Dutch still life.[6] Not all still lifes but those depicting food, 'which by their deceptive likeness necessarily excite the appetite for the things they represent'. Still life would be acceptable if we could look at it 'as a beautiful product of nature in form and colour, without being obliged to think of it as eatable'. Isn't Niépce's still life just still, yet not a still life? It is not yet full of food to be consumed by the eye. It is unlike those Dutch still lifes where 'unfortunately we often find, represented with deceptive naturalness, prepared and served dishes, oysters, herrings, crabs, bread and butter, beer, wine, and so forth, which is altogether to be condemned'. Thus excitement puts an end to aesthetic contemplation, and somehow, the philosopher is indeed excited against food as a pictorial genre. Food is like flesh, it is what he calls 'base sensuality', a desire to possess and consume the object. It threatens the spirituality of the image. The anima, the soul, turns into an animal.

Niépce shows us a still life before the meal. Schopenhauer discusses the scandal of our visual appetite. Proust, however, is interested in food as still life when the meal is over. In *Within a Budding Grove*, the narrator,

[6] Arthur Schopenhauer, *The World as Will and Idea*, volume one, book 3, paragraph 40. London: Routledge and Kegan Paul 1957.

still sitting at the table while it is being cleared, turns
his attention away from the view of the sea to cast
his gaze on the remains of the meal. Looking is not here
directly associated with eating but with the idle time
of the digestion that follows. The eye of the narrator
contemplates:

'…the broken gestures of the knives still lying
across one another, the swollen convexity of a discarded
napkin upon which the sun would patch a scrap of yellow
velvet, the half-empty glass which thus shewed to greater
advantage the noble sweep of its curved sides, and, in the
heart of its translucent crystal, clear as frozen daylight, a
dreg of wine, dusky but sparkling with reflected lights, the
displacement of solid objects, the transmutation of liquids
by the effect of light and shade, the shifting colour of the
plums which passed from green to blue and from blue to
golden yellow in the half plundered dish…'[7]

Here, the still life is neither frozen nor still. Proust's
textual still life is very much alive. He is fascinated by the
movement of the still life, by '*la vie profonde des natures
mortes*'. Translucence and light animate the objects scattered
across the tablecloth. The sentence is like a cinematic
panning on the surface of the table. This is a picture where
the only moments of stillness reside in the use of commas
that isolate certain gustative and visual events, producing
smaller pictures within the general picture of the table.

If Proust's text is decisively visual, Niépce's images are
now primarily textual. I have only seen the view from the
window at Gras in various poor reproductions in books.
The same goes for the dressed table. They are ghost images
still haunting photographic discourse. Their materiality is
uncertain, if not totally absent. They open up the narrative
of photography, just as Alberti's window and Proust's table
open onto a story.

[7] Marcel Proust, *A l'ombre des jeunes filles en fleur*, 1919, Paris Gallimard Vol. 2 of the seven part novel *A la recherché du temps perdu* (*In Search of Lost Time*). English translation: *Within a Budding Grove*, part 2, p. 235. London: Chatto & Windus, 1949.

**Ewa Axelrad**

40    *INODOROUS* 2009
Inkjet print

52-53    *SOLUTION* 2010
Mixed media
Dimensions variable

ewa.axelrad@yahoo.com
www.ewa-axelrad.com

**Stuart Bailes**

04    *The Movement of Things (Photograph I)*
C-type print
81 x 101.6 cm

07    *The Movement of Things (Photograph II)*
Black-and-white fibre-based hand print
127 x 160 cm

60    *Flank*
Black-and-white fibre-based hand print
25.4 x 30 cm

stuartbailes@gmail.com
www.stuartbailes.com / www.halsilver.com

**Joshua Bilton**

41    *Revolt in Owiu*
C-Type print
76 x 102 cm

42    *Buckle*
C-Type print
100 x 124 cm

51    *Buckle*, detail
C-Type print
74 x 100 cm

Joshua.bilton@googlemail.com
www.joshbilton.com / www.halsilver.com

**Savinder Bual**

08    *Myriorama*
Film still
Dimensions variable

11    *Follis Arboreus*
Film still
Dimensions variable

67    *Follis Paluster*
Film still
Dimensions variable

savinderbual@yahoo.co.uk
www.savinderbual.com / www.halsilver.com

**Sidsel Christensen**

30    *Light Girls*
Video still, Video DV-PAL
16:9 ratio. Dimensions variable

31    *About The Light Surface of*
*Josephine Ditlev*
Video still, Video DV-PAL
16:9 ratio. Dimensions variable

57    *Documentation from the performance*
*'Conversations with the Other Side'*
Video still, Video DV-PAL
16:9 ratio. Dimensions variable.

sidsel.c@gmail.com
www.sidselchristensen.com / www.halsilver.com

**Diana Fiedler**

12    *Interior #1. Interior constructed from the*
*exterior of a housing estate tower block*
C-type Lambda print
100 × 300 cm

13    *Unit. Interior constructed from the*
*exterior of a housing estate tower block.*
C-type Lambda print
100 × 100 cm

58    *Interior #1.* Installation view

koza@dianafiedler.com
www.dianafiedler.com

**Valerie Furnham**

44   *Propulsion*
Video stills from installation

64   *Fe2O3 = PLXNA2 = Anxiety*
Video still from installation

82   *Scratch test = 1→2→4→8→16→32→∞*
*(Anticipation)*
Video still from installation

valfurnham@yahoo.co.uk
www.valeriefurnham.com

**Noemie Goudal**

36   *Passage from the series Island*
C-type Lambda print
140 x 111 cm

37   *Les Amants (Cascade)*
C-type Lambda print
140 x 111 cm

68   *Les Amants (Chaleur)*
C-type Lambda print
140 x 111 cm

contact@noemiegoudal.com
www.noemiegoudal.com / www.halsilver.com

**Alejandro Guijarro**

09   *Sea*
C-type print
127 x 101 cm

15   *Desert*
C-type print
127 x 101cm

55   *Chopped Tomatoes*
C-type print
72 x 101 cm

alejandroguijarro@gmail.com
www.alejandroguijarro.com

**Una Hamilton Helle**

46   *Mot himmelrik*
Collage
39 x 49 cm

56   *Nekrosus*
Video still

59   *Leys*
Detail from the installation
Mixed media
25 x 50 cm

unahamiltonhelle@gmail.com
www.unahamiltonhelle.co.uk / www.halsilver.com

**Darren Harvey-Regan**

32   *Heidegger's Lizard*
C-type print
112 x 78 cm

65   *All the Logic of Which an Existence is*
*Capable – Albino Badger and Badger in a Bag*
C-type print
61 x 51 cm

77   *The Elsewhere Mouse*, detail
C-type Lambda print, folded
130 x 45 cm

darren@harveyregan.co.uk
www.harveyregan.com / www.halsilver.com

**Sarah Mei Herman**

16   *Jana and Feby, April 2009*
C-type print
70 x 90 cm

35   *Julian and Jonathan, July 2009*
C-type print
50 x 62 cm

71   *Jonathan, October 2009*
C-type print
95 x 120 cm

mail@sarahmeiherman.nl
www.sarahmeiherman.nl / www.halsilver.com

**Frederic Huska**

18    *Back to a Dead End, 1st Street Brooklyn*
C-type print

28    *Remember II*
C-type print

75    *The Corner House*
C-type print

fred@fredhuska.com
www.fredhuska.com

**Soon-Hak Hwon**

26    *History of Espace Cinq Etoiles No.5*, detail

27    *History of Espace Cinq Etoiles No.5*
Giclée Print
150 x 205 cm

81    *History of Sesame Gallery,* installation view
Giclée Print
230 x 350cm

soonhaki@gmail.com
www.soonhaki.com

**Agata Madejska**

20    *Ideogram 004, 2007–2009*
Lightjet C-type print
60 x 41.5 cm

21    *Ideogram 006, 2007–2009*
Lightjet C-type print
60 x 44.5 cm

69    *81–86, 2010*
Lightjet C-type print
119 x 162 cm

agata@madejska.eu
www.madejska.eu

**Amit Nachumi**

17    *Harvester*
C-type print
107 x 81 cm

72    *The Gate Keeper*
C-type print
107 x 81 cm

74    *Sabres*
C-type print
107 x 81 cm

amit@amitnachumi.co.uk
www.AmitNachumi.co.uk

**Darragh O'Callaghan**

22    *Brickbuilded*
Pencil on paper
Preliminary sketch for video recorded
performance

78    *Untitled*
Video still from recorded performance

79    *Jackhammered*
Pencil & watercolour on paper
Preliminary sketch for video recorded
performance

darragh.ocallaghan@network.rca.ac.uk

**Melanie Rozencwajg**

23    *Liverpool Street Station*
*Sunday 5pm - 5:30pm, Flow of People.*
Silkscreen
50 x 54cm

24    *Periphery*
Video, 4min, loop
Variable dimensions

85    *Untitled Document*
Digital print
29.7 x 42 cm

melanie.rozencwajg@gmail.com
www.me-ro.com / www.halsilver.com

**Norma-Louise Thallon**

43    *Downstairs at the King's Head*
    *(18 Minutes to Performance)*
    C-type Lambda print
    76 x 102 cm

43    *Downstairs at the King's Head*
    *(6 Minutes to Performance)*
    C-type Lambda print
    76 x 102 cm

84    *Become a Master of Disguise*
    Large Format Silverprint
    60 x 50cm

norma.thallon@network.rca.ac.uk
www.normathallon.com

**Luke Turner**

38    *The Annunciation, Sandro Botticelli*
    C-type Lambda print
    190.5 x 152.4 cm

39    *The Mocking of Christ, Fra Angelico*
    C-type Lambda print
    190.5 x 152.4 cm

61    *Untitled (in collaboration with*
    *Nastja Rönkkö)*
    Polaroid
    8.5 x 10.8 cm

luke.turner@network.rca.ac.uk
www.luketurner.com

**Lauren Winsor**

45    *Frôler*
    Fibre-based silver gelatin print
    106 x 170cm

63    *$20^2$*
    From the series *f/216*
    Fibre-based silver gelatin print
    92 x 142cm

83    *Automatic Poiesis*
    Fibre-based silver gelatin print
    50 x 65cm

lauren.winsor@network.rca.ac.uk
www.laurenwinsor.co.uk

## ACKNOWLEDGEMENTS

Published by
Royal College of Art
Kensington Gore
London
SW7 2EU

+44 (0)20 7590 4414

info@rca.ac.uk
www.rca.ac.uk

Copyright © 2010 Royal College of Art,
the authors for the text and the artists for
the photographs and stills

ISBN – 978-1-907342-07-3

Designed by Sophie Dutton, Hannah Montague
and Joseph Pochodzaj

Editor Rut Blees Luxemburg
Copy-editor Helen Wire
Project Co-ordinator Claire Smithson
Translator Jared Stark (translation of
Jean-Luc Nancy's text from French into English)

Printed by Push

Printed on Challenger Offset and Regency Gloss

Typeset in Bembo and LTC Tourist Gothic

Thanks to

The academic staff of the Photography Department:
Professor Olivier Richon, Hermione Wiltshire, Peter Kennard, Sarah Jones,
Rut Blees Luxemburg, Yve Lomax, Francette Pacteau, Stuart Croft,
Nigel Rolfe, Darian Leader, Alexander García Düttmann, Lewin St Cyr,
Jan Naraine, Simon Ward, Kam Raoofi, George Duck, Roddy Canas and
Claire Smithson.

Roy Killen at Push for print and production

Special Thanks to

Alexander García Düttmann and Jean-Luc Nancy for their fervent
engagement with the project and their generous response to the students
invitation to participate in this book.